W9-AQV-379

CHILDREN'S THEATER IN ELEMENTARY SCHOOL

CHILDREN'S THEATER IN ELEMENTARY SCHOOL

Pierini, M. P. F.

SISTER PAUL FRANCIS PIERINI, SNJM

Art: Sister Roberta Carson, SNJM
Photography: George F. Perry

PN
3157
.P5

A Crossroad Book
The Seabury Press • New York

1977

The Seabury Press
815 Second Avenue
New York, N.Y.   10017

Printed in the United States of America

Library of Congress Cataloging in Publication Data

Pierini, Mary Paul Francis.
  Children's theater in elementary school.

  1. Children's plays--Presentation, etc.
2. Drama in education. I. Title.
PN3157.P5   372.6'6   76-54641
ISBN 0-8164-0342-2

To all who bring wonder and delight

into the lives of boys and girls

We are grateful to the following friends for permission to reprint materials:

George F. Perry, Master of Photography, photographs

James Haran, "The Sorcerer's Apprentice"

Sister Marie Fleurette, IHM, and Sister Denise, IHM, "Rumpelstiltskin"

Contents

Preface 9

I.   WHY CHILDREN'S THEATER 13

II. WARMING-UP EXERCISES 19

"What-to-Look-for-in-a-Play" 23

III. THE PLAY

Choosing a script 31

Workshop Objectives 35

Tryouts 38

Rehearsals 43

Dress Rehearsals 48

Day of Performance 57

IV. MUSICAL PLAY 61

V.   MATERIALS 70

PREFACE

This book has been written in response to pleas and cries of "help" from
many teachers, parents, and students who are firmly committed to the values
of children's theater. Their own delightful and rewarding experiences want
sharing with children in the elementary schools, they say. To realize
their desire, however, they seek help and direction. May their patience
find some reward in this publication which offers practical helps and suggestions in a combination of pictures, art work, and script.

There are a number of excellent books now available on the philosophy
of children's theater, the kinds of plays children like, and script writing.
Therefore, this book in no way purports to repeat what has already been
written and in considerable detail. What is intended here is to share with
the reader actual materials which have worked successfully in productions
for and with children in the elementary schools. Every phase of the step-
by-step operation from techniques for tryouts, rehearsal, and propmaking to
dress rehearsal, performances, and touring is covered. There are sample
guides for selecting plays, "cutting" scripts, casting, setting up crews,
and publicity. From this variety of learning aids the reader may confidently
begin to introduce children to the best in children's theater.

In drama, to act is not to be, but to do. Hence, it is greatly to be
desired that an understanding of and enthusiasm for this art for boys and
girls will encourage the reader to "try your wings" in children's theater.
So many children will never see or participate in live theater unless you
begin to lead them --- today!

WHY CHILDREN'S THEATER?

WHY CHILDREN'S THEATER?

When today's children appear to be so effortlessly, inexpensively, and satisfactorily entertained by television, it is entirely logical, perhaps, to pose the question, "Why go to all the trouble and time of doing children's theater with elementary school children?" There are, of course, many possible answers; only a few of them should be sufficient to establish the value of live theater for children, also its function and place in education.

If to educate is to "draw out," then this is precisely what live children's theater is designed to do --- stimulate a child's extremely active imagination; give young senses objects worthy of attracting them; involve awakening emotions with the beautiful and the good; and lead growing intellects to grasp, pleasurably, the true. In live children's theater all this is done under wisely controlled conditions and in a way calculated to give boys and girls the kind and quality of experience to which they can fully respond; so fully, in fact, that they will live these experiences over and over again. Which adult does not recall the magic hours he knew, as a child, when he vicariously guessed Rumpelstiltskin's name, wore Cinderella's slipper, danced the Fairy Queen waltz, and even rode Huck Finn's raft?

When I speak of "wisely controlled conditions" which dispose children to get the most from seeing a play, I am speaking first of all about getting them ready to see it. There is an enormous difference for a child between leaving the dinner table to sit down alone, or with one or two other children, to watch T.V. (even if it is that rarity, a good children's play), and dressing to go out to a play, having his own ticket, finding his special seat among other children (behaving better than usual, perhaps); finally, sensing that this is an EVENT important enough to have his mother and father take time to bring him a long way to the theater, even sit with him through this play as they rarely do before television. In a word, the child who comes to a live children's play is, when the curtain goes up, psychologically ready to pay special attention to what he will see, for he has reason to believe that it has to be important to have commanded such preparation on his part and such attention from adults.

But what is it he will see? Not figures on a screen, but live actors, often children of his own age, doing things he may not be able to do, but which he would like to believe he can do: save the princess, find the bad man, uphold the law, protect little children from evil witches, be unafraid of danger, dance and sing so beautifully that he will try to do both himself once he is quite alone again in his room.

As a child's interest in plays increases, he will, if allowed to follow the pied-pipers of dialogue, pantomime, color, music, and dance, develop

13

an independence and awareness of his ability to think and judge them for himself. Such a child is not likely, later on, to be among those who are "looking for their identity." Once in "Many Moons," when the princess exclaimed, "I loathe prunes," an alert seven-year-old in the audience un-hesitatingly announced at the top of her voice, "So do I." Neither the princess nor anyone in the audience thought this funny. All knew that prunes are no laughing matter. Here was a proper, instantaneous, if not unusual, understanding between character and child --- an understanding which the rest of the audience respected.

To watch the wholehearted, genuine, unrestrained responses of children to a well-acted story, is somehow to catch a glimpse of the mystery of growth: the magician's seed springs up before one's eyes --- branch, blossom, leaf, flower --- for an effective and successful children's play touches to life the whole child --- intellect, senses, imagination, emotions. Whether he is aware of it or not, this child is storing up memories while he lives a play, valuable memories he will cherish into adulthood. This does not mean, however, that a children's play may not be enjoyed by adults. What C. S. Lewis has said about children's stories is equally applicable to children's plays:

> ...I never met THE WIND IN THE WILLOWS until I was in my late twenties, and I do not think I have enjoyed it less on that account. I am almost inclined to set up as a canon that a children's story which is enjoyed only by children is a bad children's story. The good ones last. A waltz which you can like only when you are waltzing is a bad waltz.

This truth finds support in the type of comment adults often make after seeing a good children's play: "It captured for me a whole world of happy memories." Sometimes it is the simplicity of the story, the poetic truth contained in it, the beauty of a setting, or a blend of all these which evokes these memories. For example, children and adults alike can learn something from LITTLE BLACK SAMBO:

> Mumbo, the mother: Come, you don't really need those things.
>
> Sambo, the son: Don't you really, truly need a thing when you want, want, want it?
>
> Mumbo: You must learn to want what you can have, Honey.

Or from RUMPELSTILTSKIN:

> Rumpelstiltskin: I have come to claim your promise.
>
> Queen: I had forgotten all about it.
>
> Rumpelstiltskin: Things don't end because you forget them.

Over and above the important and lasting effects of good children's
theater on its audience, there are also rewards for both director and
actors. To elicit a genuine dramatic experience in a child by means of
children's theater, every effort must be exerted to select a play within
the range of that child's understanding and to produce this play in such
a way as to evoke response. To meet this challenge no effort is too great
if it results in one hour of beauty, laughter, joy, and significant excitment for a child; of this fact, a director and cast must be wholeheartedly
convinced. To assure such an experience for children, a director must be
ready to cut, rewrite, or make additions to a script during or immediately
after a performance. As outstanding playwright Charlotte Chorpenning has
said: "Children's plays are not written. They are rewritten." Producing
such plays, then, is not just a matter of "putting on a little show."
With such an attitude, any show is as good as lost.

For the actors there is always the excitment of stimulating and retain-
ing hard-won children's attention. Pantomime, gesture, facial expression,
and body movement play such an important part in this process that they
must learn to use each deftly, precisely, and convincingly. This demands
control which is not easily come by, therefore not attained successfully
by all. Learning to play a scene "broadly" without its becoming "slaps-
stick"; skillfully pacing episodes so as to prevent restlessness in the
young audience without destroying the overall movement and timing; pro-
jecting lines and articulating dialogue so that the child hears distinctly
and understands every word that is being said --- these and other skills
demand a kind of sensitivity and self-discipline which are recognized and
generously rewarded by children far more spontaneously and wholeheartedly
than by adults.

Of all the arts, drama appeals most strongly to children and affects
them most fully and immediately. Whoever has observed little boys and
girls sitting spellbound in a theater, oblivious to all but the story
being acted out before their eyes, can have no doubt of this. If the plays
they see are the kind of plays a responsible director and cast should produce especially for children, then,children's theater can be a powerful
antidote to T.V. and a sorely needed force for untold good today.

WARMING-UP EXERCISES

WARMING-UP EXERCISES

Before children begin to rehearse a play, it is both necessary and prof-
itable to exercise them in activities which will free them in body movements and use of voices. Characterization is enacting a role so that the
audience believes in its reality and individuality. To give character to
a role means to endow that role with the mental faculties, the emotion,
the peculiarities of personality, the physical aspect, and the personal
mannerisms which are the integral part of a particular human being. No
small task for anyone, let alone beginners. Therefore, children need to
"try on" various kinds of body movement using the whole body, individual
parts -- face, hands, feet, etc. -- walks, postures, etc., to express a
particular character. If plot is what the characters do, characterization shows why they do it.

SUGGESTIONS

Different people may ring your doorbell. Show us in (a) pantomine,
(b) with movement and dialogue each of the following characters. Establish
age, sex, a specific peculiarity, and bring the situation to a conclusion:

   1. Old man who has lost his way.

   2. Lady who has locked her car key inside her car.

   3. Boy scout who is trying to sell his last three boxes of cookies.

Swishety, swishety, swishety, shwby,
I'm grown up! Who am I? (fatigued baseball pitcher; King Arthur dis-
                         covering Excalibur; spaceman landing on a new
                         planet)

Fiddle, dee de! Fiddle dee, da!
A million things in this world to see.
A king, a giant, a lion, a tree (change names, as you wish).
Who in the world, would you like to be?   Show us!

Show by body movement and facial expression the age, sex, and feelings
of individuals in these group situations:

1. Airport: making a ticket exchange; having bags checked
2. Church: late entrance; participating in service
3. School: (Do, as preschooler; as high schooler; as college
   student)
   a. Late entrance to class
   b. Working problem on blackboard
   c. Eating lunch

Select a Mother Goose rhyme. Present it in three ways, using movement
and dialogue:

1. As an interpretation
2. As interpreted by a first grader
3. As interpreted by a jazzy teenager
4. As interpreted by a sophisticated college student

Humorous cartoon: Children look and read lines; then, improvise the situation bringing the cartoon "to life."

Magazine pictures or paintings (Rockwell's, "The Gossips"). Children
study pictures or paintings; select individual in the picture and reproduce in
movement and dialogue. Freeze, as if in a picture; "melt" and show what
happened after the picture-taking.

Parts of body: Stand behind a table. Make feet (hands, feet and hands)
express these emotions:

I'm tired walking.
I hope I get an "A."
Home at last.
I hate school.

IMPROVISATIONS: spontaneous, spur-of-the moment actions and dialogue.
As action is what characters do, so dialogue is what characters say as
they become involved in the emotions of a situation.

Using the following dialogue, present it in the following ways:

    1. Straight.
    2. Invent two characters and a specific situation using same dialogue.
    3. Keep the same characters. Change the situation.
    4. Change the characters. Keep the same situation.

Dialogue: A. Hello.
             B. Hello.
             A. Well.
             B. Well, what?
             A. How are things?
             B. Just about as usual.
             A. I didn't expect to find you here.
             B. But you have. Of course, I could say the same about you.
             A. Are you going to be busy from now until dinner?
             B. No, not exactly busy.
             A. Would you like to talk for a while?
             B. I might, for a while anyway.
             A. Right.
             B. Right.

Three minutes situations:

Two old friends come to the park to play checkers. The wife of one of them
comes and tells her husband to come home.

Tom Sawyer has been told to paint the fence. He convinces his friend to do
it for him.

Opening line: "Look, who is coming to our class room."

A service station attendant waits on a customer and overcharges her by mistake.

The following playlet, "What-To-Look-For-In-A-Play," serves a double
purpose: first, it provides a vehicle within which girls and boys may
stretch their imaginations in movement and voice in an improvisational
way as they familiarize themselves with some fundamentals and language
involved in a play: such as, a story told in action; beginning-middle-
end high points; dialogue; gesture; movement; key words; characters;
props. And second, it may serve as an excellent introduction to audiences,
particularly those which include boys and girls who have never experienced
"live children's theater." The varieties of ways in which this playlet
may be interpreted have no other limitation than the imaginations and
ingenuities of director and cast!

WHAT-TO-LOOK-FOR-IN-A-PLAY Demonstration

Characters: Neuter #1 ...... Gay, youthful
                   Neuter #2 ...... Agile, graceful
                   Neuter #3 ...... Happily "sinister"
                   Neuter #4 ...... Very "motherly"

(All characters enter to music dancing and carrying large suitcase.   Part of
the movement consists of opening the suitcase stage center and taking out set
and prop items: folded-up tree which is opened and placed stage right, some-
what back; folded-up lamp post which is set down stage left; cobweb (bare
umbrella with yarn tacked on to look like web) is placed under tree; props
(bow for Girl, apron for Mother, antennae for Spider, butterfly net for Girl)
are placed where Characters may put them on quickly to begin play.)

Music fades out as Characters stand in straight line facing audience.

#4: (to audience) Good morning!

     This is a "What-To-Look-For-In-A-Play" demonstration (she looks at

     characters who stand in "Neuter" positions).

     And we are going to tell you what is in a play, and show you what to look

     for!

Now,

     a play is a STORY

                    TOLD IN ACTION

     and what you look for is

                    THE STORY,

                         and WHAT THE STORY TELLS YOU, and

                         THE ACTION THAT TELLS IT.

You can always recognize a story because it always has a <u>BEGINNING</u>,

<u>MIDDLE</u>, and an <u>END</u>.

Now, you all know the beginning, because it always begins...

#1: ONCE UPON A TIME (steps forward, speaks, returns to Neuter position).

#4:   And you can always tell the ending because it always ends...

#2:   HAPPILY EVER AFTER (Steps forward, speaks, returns to Neuter position).

      (#4 looks "pleased" at #1 and #2. #3 beckons for attention.)

#4:   Oh! The middle...

      The middle part of a story is WHAT THE STORY TELLS YOU!

      (#3 nods in approval, returns to Neuter position).

#4:   It can tell you by DIALOGUE (steps to front).

#3:   Dialogue occurs when two people talk to each other.

      I'm going to talk to you (points to child in audience). Hello!

      What's your name? How are you? (If one child does not respond

      work out other dialogue with someone else.)

#4:   The middle part of the story can be told to you by GESTURE.

#2:   (Yawns, scratches head, recognizes audience, waves! Return to

      Neuter position.)

#4:   Or MOVEMENT.

#3:   (Steps back in, turns cartwheels into Neuter position.)

#4:   Dialogue, gesture, and movement relate the ACTION, and action is

      WHAT IS TOLD BY THE CHARACTERS USING EQUIPMENT.

      So...we need equipment, in this case

            a spider web (#3 points to web)

                  and a forest (#2 points to tree)

                        and a house (#1 points to lamp post).

Then we need COLOR.

      Here we have BLUE (#3 points to costume, pulls out ends of skirt)

                  RED (#2 points to costume, pulls out ends of skirt)

                  YELLOW (#1 points to costume, pulls out ends of skirt).

Oh, and GREEN (#4 points to costume, pulls out ends of skirt. Now all

four characters are standing in straight line facing audience. They
have ends of skirts in hands. They take Neuter positions again.)

#4: Next, we need words. (Each number turns to one on right with sweeping
gesture of greeting.)

#3: Hello.

#2: Howdy.

#1: How are you?

#4: Fine (note of finality).

Let's see, we've got equipment, color, words ---

All we need next are CHARACTERS

 (Walking back to lamp post, looks back and says)

with SOMETHING to say,

(Characters put on costumes: #1 - Bow; takes "butterfly net" -- GIRL

#2 - Pins on wings (scarves) -- BUTTERFLY

#3 - Puts on antennae (pipecleaners on
                                band) -- SPIDER

#4 - Puts on apron -- MOTHER.)

MOTHER: Once upon a time in a faraway land, there lived a mother (positions),

GIRL: a little girl (positions, freezes),

BUTTERFLY: a butterfly (takes position, turns back to audience),

SPIDER: and a big black and blue spider (takes position, turns back to audience).

MOTHER: Something has to be done about this yard. It is so untidy.

        (Enter Girl carrying butterfly net.)

        What are you doing?

GIRL: It's such a beautiful day. I'm off to catch butterflies.

MOTHER: Be sure not to go into the forest. You know the big black and blue

        spider lives there, and you might get caught in his web.

25

GIRL: I would never go in there, Mother.

MOTHER: All right, dear. Have fun and be home early. (Waves goodby,
           goes into house, upstage, turns back.)

[Girl looks for butterflies. .Soon the Butterfly begins to flutter near her.
(music) She tries to catch him and follows him into the Forest.]

GIRL: Oh, that butterfly is too tricky. I might as well go home.
           (Butterfly gets caught in spider web. Girl tries to find her way
           out of Forest.)

GIRL: But I don't know where I am! I MUST be in the Forest (frightened).
           There must be a way out.

BUTTERFLY:Please help me, help me get untangled from this web.

GIRL: But I'm lost and my Mother's waiting for me. (Enter Spider -- faces
           front, looks sinister.)

SPIDER: On look! What a tasty supper I'll have tonight. (Butterfly reacts
           frantically.)

GIRL: The Spider! Hold still so I can free you. (Unsuccessful at her
           efforts, Girl gives up and is chased by Spider -- THE CHASE is done
           in stylistic movement.)
           (Freeze as spider almost catches Girl.)

MOTHER: (comes to front) My, I wonder where my little Girl could be. It
           is late. (Chase continues. Spider is tricked and caught. Girl
           frees Butterfly.)

GIRL: But I'm lost. I'll never get home!

BUTTERFLY:I'll lead you out of the Forest. Follow me. (Music -- dancing
           Butterfly leads Girl to her home.)

GIRL: Mother!

MOTHER: Oh, I'm so happy you are home. I was so worried. Where have you been?

GIRL: I was chasing a Butterfly and got lost in the Forest, and the big

Black and Blue Spider chased me, and this good Butterfly helped me

find my way home after I freed her from the Spider's web. I'll never

go into the Forest again. If it wasn't for my new friend, I might

never have gotten out.

(Mother, Butterfly, Girl join hands. Butterfly breaks loose, goes to Spider,

playfully brings him into the circle and all join in a "Friendship Dance.")

Characters put props into suitcase, wave, and exit dancing to same music used

for entrance.

THE PLAY

CHOOSING A SCRIPT

A script must be considered from the viewpoints of both the actors and
the audience. The actors need a play which provides opportunities for
them to project characters to bring a story alive; and the audience
must be swept up in the lively story which the characters tell. Three
criteria for selecting a script should be considered:

* It should present a direct, simple story line in dialogue.
* It should provide action.
* It should include a "chase."

It should present a direct, simple story line in dialogue.

Children like to see a favorite and familiar story come to life. It
attracts their attention and holds their interest. However, it sustains
their participation to the highest degree when the story follows a direct
line of development. A brief, but clear beginning sets the scene and
introduces the characters who become involved in a series of events leading
to a high point or climax. The end follows quickly. For example, in the
opening scene of James Haran's "The Sorcerer's Apprentice" the Elf talks
directly to the audience and quickly sets the scene and situation.

Scene: The Sorcerer's Workshop

        Elf appears!

     Elf: Hello boys and girls. Do you know what I am? Do you?
           I'm an Elf and I live here in this Sorcerer's Workshop.
           Now, there are good sorcerers and bad sorcerers, and my
           master is a good Sorcerer. He is always trying to help
           people out. He makes it rain so the crops will grow, or
           cures people of toothaches, ingrown toenails, and things
           like that. He is really very nice, but (looks around)
           you know, he's getting old and cranky, and sometimes he
           gets cross at me -- and makes me disappear! Oh yes, he's
           very clever at that. But most of the time he gets angry
           at his little apprentice, that's his helper, who is
           studying to be a sorcerer himself. So far he hasn't done
           very well. To tell you the truth I think he's a little
           bit lazy. Oh, oh, here he comes.

And so this script is off to an immediate and clear start. An imaginative creature, the Elf, talks directly to the audience about two main characters in the story. The magic powers of the Sorcerer have been introduced and the important point about the "lazy" Apprentice suggests that his weakness may just lead him into trouble. Key names and key actions are introduced. The actor's business is to bring the speeches alive to the audience, making his character clear as he does so.

It should provide action.

Both as actors and as audience children respond most enthusiastically to action. A script that is "talky" loses them and, of course, if it is "too talky" will prompt the audience to be inattentive -- a catastrophe for the players! Movement and its complement, the "frozen picture," inform without words. The actor uses movement (whole body, parts of body) to communicate both his character and the story line. His speaking lines and his movements, therefore, work together, one just as important as the other.

At specific moments, the actors "freeze" their positions, holding them long enough so that the audience sees a picture, as one might stop to look at a picture in a storybook. For example, in "The Sorcerer's Apprentice," following the Elf's introduction to the audience, the Apprentice and Wizard enter:

Movement

Apprentice enters slowly, dragging old, untidy straw broom which he uses as a cane.

Elf skips around Apprentice, leaps into air, and lands at feet of Apprentice, blocking his way.

Apprentice: Hello, Elf.

Elf: Hello.
    What are you doing today?

Elf does somersault facing audience.

Apprentice: I'm supposed to clean up the workshop, and fill the cauldron. But I'm tired already and haven't even started.

Elf's face saddens as he mimics Apprentice's slow speech, turning head side to side.

Frozen picture: Apprentice slouches on broom handle. Elf collapses with feet up in the air.

Elf: (to audience) See, I told you he was lazy!

These specific body movements of Elf mimicking the apprentice communicate to the audience the boy's attitude toward work, which later gets him into trouble with the Witch of Thunder Mountain. The "frozen picture" underscores the Apprentice's laziness and becomes a vivid memory for recall later.

It should include a "chase."

As the story line builds to a main climax, it is important to provide moments of action along the way which encourage physical movement from the audience -- moments when their applause, laughter, body wiggling which release pent-up energy may be exercised legitimately. Then, comes the "chase" -- that exciting moment when characters actually chase one another. For example, the Apprentice says the magic words which the Witch tells him to say to the broom if he wants to get his work done.

Apprentice: Ali kazam, ali kazoo.
Broom, do what I tell you to do.
Broom, move. (The broom "sprouts" arms.)
Broom, pick up those buckets. (Broom picks up buckets, one in each hand.)
Broom, get water and fill the cauldron.
(Broom slowly begins to follow directions. Softly, and gradually louder, the music of "The Sorcerer's Apprentice" by Paul Dukas plays.)
It's doing just what I tell it. That's it. Fill the cauldron. Fill the cauldron. (Broom moves faster, in and out, in and out, bringing in buckets of water, filling the cauldron.)
Oh, I am getting tired. I think I'll sit down and rest here. (Dozes off as Broom keeps working -- faster, faster.)
Fillll... the... (goes to sleep).

(Witch rises from behind cauldron and dances around, sinks down at base of cauidron as Apprentice awakens.)

What's this? Why, there's water on the floor; the cauldron. The broom. I must stop it. Oh, what a mess this place is. Now, my Master, will surely punish me!
Stop, Broom (chases broom), stop Broom. I, your master, command you to stop. Broom, please stop. Oh, what a wicked Witch, she told me how to start the broom, but didn't tell me how to stop it!
Broom, you've got to stop -- stop! I know! The axe! I'll stop the broom with the axe. (He gets axe, chases broom off stage. Chopping is heard.)

(Apprentice returns) There, that's that. But look at the mess! How am
                I going to get rid of the water? (Hears noise). What is
                that noise? It sounds like -- it can't be... (two brooms
                enter with buckets of water). Now there are two...oh...
                (chases brooms). What am I going to do? The water is get-
                ting higher and -- I can't swim. Help!

     This scene certainly provides many opportunities for the audience to
respond to the questions of the Apprentice, to react physically and
audibly when he chases the brooms. It is a genuine "chase" sequence.

WORKSHOP OBJECTIVES

To introduce children to the various concepts of children's theater, including characterization (voice, movement, dialogue), stylization (acting techniques which include face front, large movements, "freeze" or hold pictures, key story-line words emphasized) and storytelling (beginning, middle, end, with small scenes leading to climax and all leading to main climax and quick ending).

To offer opportunities through workshop sessions for each child to grow both as an individual and as a member of a group in participation, in creativity, and in performance and/or creation of set, props, costume, makeup, etc. Hopefully, this growth will give him an appreciation of the work involved throughout the production, an understanding of the mechanics of a production (including the roles of director, cast, crews), and a rewarding experience in sharing talents with an audience.

MEETING PLACE

Auditorium or large room. Use floor of auditorium if stage is high or "boxy." There should be room enough for easy movement and entrance and exit areas.

Crews meet in their own "workroom" where materials are available and may be stored after each session.

PERFORMANCES

Two or more, so that cast and crews experience: (1) responses of different audiences; (2) rewards of sharing their talents, time, and energies; and (3) reactions to their own accomplishments.

DIRECTOR

Main director and three co-directors (or leaders). The latter may be selected from among children.

WORKSHOP MEETINGS

Six (6) one-and-a-half or two-hour sessions (minimum).
Cast is responsible for learning roles.
Main director directs script.
Assistant director has charge of movement.
Co-director guides props, makeup and sound crews.
Co-director guides set, costumes, makeup and light crews.

FIRST MEETING

Directors and children meet in large room.
One director briefly acquaints girls and boys with script.
Another director introduces importance of various crews.
Another director explains "tryout sheets."
Fourth director explains "reading" and obligation involved in accepting
    a part in the production (regular attendance is essential as production
    will be limited in time). It is to be noted here that too many
    rehearsals and/or rehearsals spread over an extended period of time
    deaden spontaneity --- a "must" if children's theater is to attract
    and sustain a young audience.
Children fill out "try out" sheets.

TRYOUT SHEET

Name_____Grade_____Telephone Number_____

I am interested in (check 1st, 2nd, 3rd choices)

_____ acting

_____ set

_____ props

_____ makeup

_____ costume

_____ lights

_____ sound

Instrument(s) I play:_____

Other plays I have been in:

Points to keep in mind as you tryout for a role:

Voice _____

Volume _____

Characterization _____

Movement _____

(On the bottom section of this sheet, each director writes in specific comments
which will help him in selecting a child for a role. These comments may be
shared with individual children at a later date.)

TRYOUTS

Move quickly.
Children trying out announce their names and part they are reading.
First, ask for "volunteers"; then, call out names.
Call back of children directors wish to hear again.
Directors quickly mark names of children after character's name.
    Particular note is made of audibility and expressiveness in voice,
    body movement, interplay with other characters.
Provide short time for children to read over material. Then begin.

Selection for tryout is taken from "The Sorcerer's Apprentice," by
James Haran.

Apprentice: Hello, Elf.

Elf: Hello. What are you doing today?

Apprentice: I'm supposed to clean up this workshop and fill the magic
              cauldron, but I'm tired already and I haven't started.

Elf:(aside)   See, I told you he was lazy.

Apprentice: Oh, I wish I had a day off.

Elf: You don't want to be a sorcerer, do you.

Apprentice: What do you mean I don't want to be a sorcerer? Of course
              I do, but my master won't teach me any tricks. All I get to
              do is sweep the floor and fill the cauldron. I'm so tired of
              filling the cauldron that I...those buckets of water are heavy.

Elf: Well, you know, you're an apprentice and all apprentices have
              to work. Now why don't you...

Apprentice: (imitating him)...do your work and then maybe he'll teach you
              some tricks. I know --- I know. He won't teach me anything.
              All he makes me do is work. I'd run away but then he'd fire me
              and I'd never get to be a sorcerer.

Elf: I guess you want to be a sorcerer at that.

Apprentice: More than anything else in the world.

Sorcerer: Oh, ho, so this is how you get your work done, is it! The
              floor is dirty, the cauldron is empty!
              (Sees Elf) So you've been talking to that pixie, again. I'll
              take care of that, right now.

Apprentice: Please, sir, it wasn't his fault. You see...

Sorcerer: Silence!
              Come here, bad influence.
              Now, ali kazam, ali pazo,
              I shake my cloth and away you go. (Elf disappears)

Apprentice: Where did he go?

Sorcerer: Never mind, now get back to work, you lazy boy.

A selection, such as this one, provides a sequence with three main characters.
It allows for the one who is "trying out" to express the character in voice
and movement and to relate that character to the others in the scene. On
the other hand, the director is able to hear different voices and see sizes
and body movement, and also, to switch readers easily.

Main director and co-directors select cast and crew members while children fill out information cards (see below).

On blackboard (or large sheet of paper) write in names of those selected for crews, then the names of the cast.

Each child is given a script as his name appears.

Scripts are to be returned at the "post mortem."

Each child receives a list of meeting times, days and dates, with "deadlines."

> Deadlines: cast to memorize lines
> props ready
> set ready
> makeup try-on
> sound
> costume try-on
> full dress rehearsal (second meeting from last one)
> final dress rehearsal (with some audience members present)

If there is time, cast and crews go to designated areas: cast reads script; crews begin plans.

> CAST: write in blocking; underscore key words; note props, movement, dance/song.

> CREWS: read script marking (listing) materials they are responsibile for; write deadlines; select one responsible.

The first meeting is crucial to the success of the entire workshop and production. It should be well-planned in order that all details may be covered in the alotted time. Each child leaves knowing the organization and responsibilities involved.

INFORMATION CARD

Telephone number_____

Name_____ Age_____ Grade_____

Address_____
                                                                zip

School_____ Address_____

Teacher_____ Hobbies_____

PRODUCTION

CREW:

COSTUME
1. _____ 4. _____
2. _____ 5. _____
3. _____ 6. _____

SOUND
1. _____ 4. _____
2. _____ 5. _____
3. _____

LIGHTS
1. _____
2. _____
3. _____

PROPS
1. _____ 5. _____
2. _____ 6. _____
3. _____ 7. _____
4. _____

PUBLICITY
1. _____
2. _____ 4. _____
3. _____ 5. _____
        6. _____

CAST:
1. _____
2. _____
3. _____
4. _____
5. _____
6. _____
7. _____
8. _____
9. _____

MAKE-UP
1. _____ 5. _____
2. _____ 6. _____
3. _____ 7. _____
4. _____ 8. _____

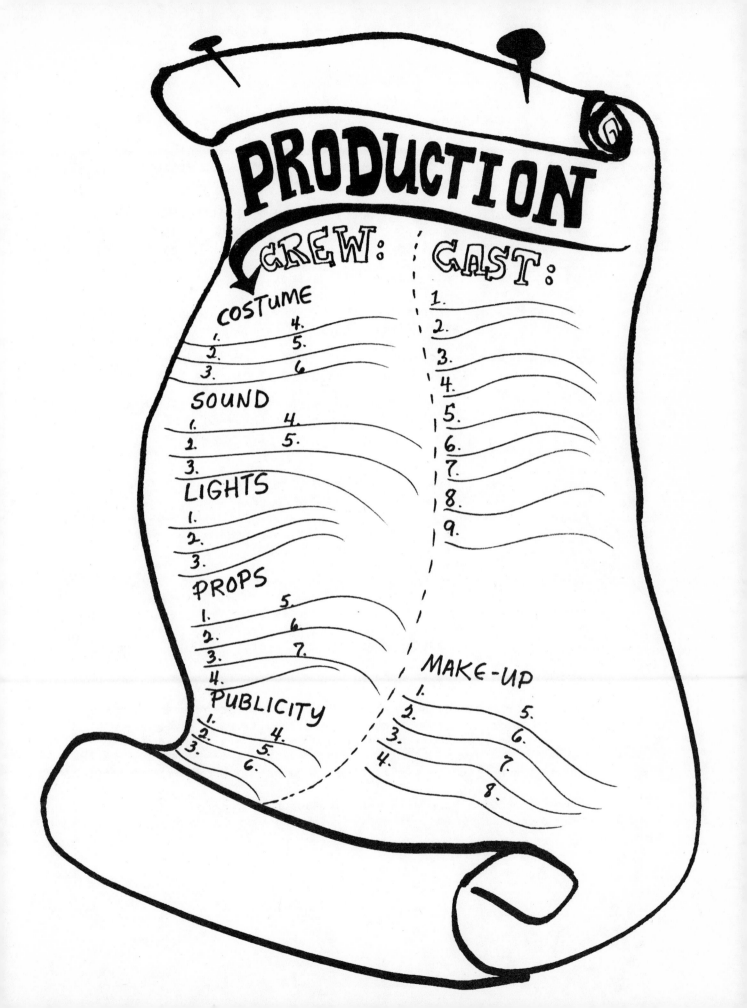

CAST: working on characters

Those with specific lines and movement should be given exercises in Creative Dramatics until they begin to create movements which they do with ease and which contribute to the story.

    Provide improvisations wherein the boys and girls realize the importance of "staying in character," becoming a part of a total scene in order to sustain the continuity of a story line.

        Movement exercises: whole body, parts of body. For example,

        Whole body: Elf appearing and disappearing, turning somersaults; jumping, skipping, etc.

        Parts of body: Sorcerer using his hands to perform magic tricks; holding his head high as if he wore a tall hat.

                        Apprentice walking with his shoulders stooped, dragging his legs because he is so tired.

    Distinctive characteristics:

        Walks: Lively Elf; magestic Sorcerer; smart Apprentice

        Facial expression: Elf making fun of Apprentice; Apprentice wishing he were a sorcerer; Sorcerer performing an unusual trick.

        Characters observe one another; mirror movements precisely.

        Other exercises: using face -- express joy, anger, sadness, fear
                            using feet -- express laziness, majesty, happiness
                            using upper body -- express delight, disappointment

        Improvise activity with each of above emotions:

            Two brooms meet and express "joy" in different ways.
            Two elfs meet and express "fear" in different ways.
            Two sorcerers meet and express "delight" in different ways.

        Add dialogue: (voice first, then language) to above improvisations.

        Repeat improvisations with musical background.

HAVE FUN!

REHEARSALS

SECOND MEETING

Cast: lines memorized
       work on stressing key words
       precision in movements

   Director's criticisms: emphasize "positive" as much as possible.
   Crews: work with co-directors on "deadline" materials.
   Sound: get acquainted with equipment.

IMPORTANT THAT PLAY BE REHEASED SEVERAL TIMES SO THAT CAST MEMBERS BECOME
FAMILIAR WITH LINES AND SITUATIONS.

   Crews must begin actual work on set and props so that once a deadline
is met a crew member is responsible to set up materials at each of the following
rehearsals. Cast members need to use props, particularly, as soon as possible.
Sound crew must understand that a "sound cue" is just as important as a speech
cue.

THIRD MEETING

Sound introduced, is music used.

   Crew member demonstrates.
   Cast gives sound crew "cues" for sound entrance; fade in-out.
   Cast: work on "staying in character" and "facing front." At all times,
audibility should be stressed. If the audience can not hear what is going on,
the audience becomes restless.
   Set crew: place scenery. If boxes are used, show how to handle them.
   Prop crew: demonstrate hand props. Props should be easily visible --
large, colorful. They should complement the set.
   Director's criticisms include props and sound, as well as cast.
   Comments from sound, props and set crews.
      Properly used? In right location?

FOURTH MEETING

Movements with and without music.
   Individual characters select specific walks and body movements which
clearly identify them.
   Work on pace -- fast entrances and exits.
      Movements and lines moving steadily to a climax.
   Select and work on "freeze" pictures.
   Director's criticisms.
   Comments from movement and song director(s).

Cardboard boxes
provide three
dimensional sets
and costumes.

Boxes are easily
moved, simplified
in lines, and easily
accessable.

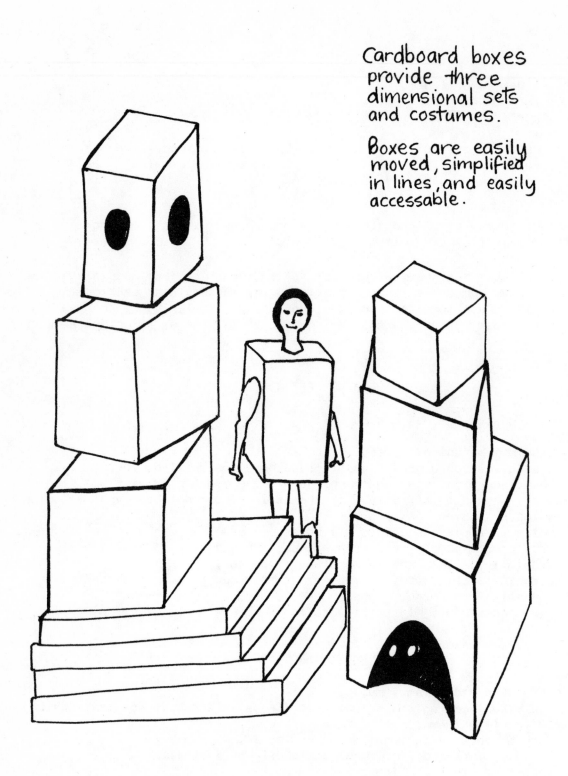

boxes may even
be used stacked
to form a tree.

DRESS REHEARSALS

FIFTH MEETING

Costumes: cast "parade" so crew may check on items --
            hat, gloves, shoes; stockings, etc.
    Cast: work on "staying in character,"
            and facing front.
            Allow facial and body movements to communicate.
    Director's criticisms.
    Comments from costume crew.

SIXTH MEETING

Full dress rehearsal
    MAKEUP: Stylized (draw on face with minimum amount of makeup;
emphasize eyes, mouth).

LIGHTS: at least one spot in addition to overhead light.
    Crews act as "audience" ti give cast a chance to respond to audience.
    Rehearse CURTAIN CALL (in character).

Director's criticisms
    Comments: co-directors and crew members
    Schedule for performances:
        Specific time for makeup, costume, check props, lights, sound
        Information regarding: taking pictures
                                "striking set"

Costume for monkey:
  black stockings for head
  masks and stuffed tails;
  brown leotard for body

54

54

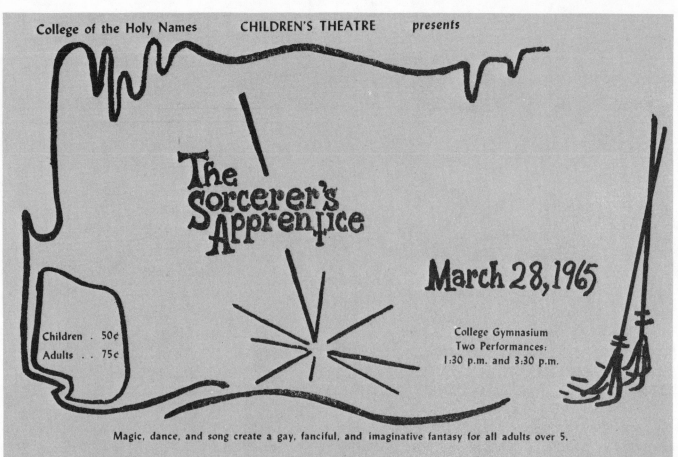

College of the Holy Names   CHILDREN'S THEATRE   presents

The Sorcerer's Apprentice

March 28, 1965

Children . 50¢
Adults . . 75¢

College Gymnasium
Two Performances:
1:30 p.m. and 3:30 p.m.

Magic, dance, and song create a gay, fanciful, and imaginative fantasy for all adults over 5.

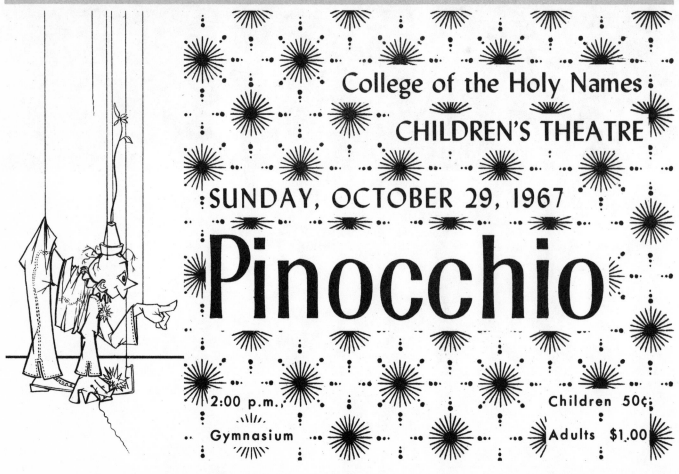

College of the Holy Names

CHILDREN'S THEATRE

SUNDAY, OCTOBER 29, 1967

Pinocchio

2:00 p.m.,

Gymnasium

Children 50¢

Adults $1.00

DAY OF PERFORMANCE

Makeup and costume crews: 1½ hours before performance
    Cast: check exits, entrances, props by 30 minutes before show.
    Sound check equipment one hour before show.
    All in places 20 minutes before audience is admitted.

    Begin "on time" allowing 5 - 10 minute wait for "late arrivals."

    After final curtain call, have lights turned on; cast and crew members
go down to chat with audience.

MEMOS TO DIRECTOR: Actors must be heard.
                      Every actor must be in character at all times.
                      Face front when delivering lines.
                      Pace lines so that pickup on cue is fast, but line
                         itself is delivered meaningfully.
                      Movement replaces verbal; therefore, it should be
                         distinct.
                      Above all, ENJOY, ENJOY telling a story to the
                         audience.

MEMOS TO CREW DIRECTORS: After reading the script, children assume specific
                      work and deadlines.
                      All materials must be available at first meeting -- card-
                         board, boxes, paint, scissors, masking and Scotch tapes,
                         stapler are basic.
                      Crews responsible for providing and putting away materials
                         needed at each rehearsal.
                      Crew members demonstrate to cast how materials are to be
                         used, worn, etc.

PICTURES: Take cast and crew pictures after first performance.
                         Members may order and pay for copies when pictures are
                         developed.
                      After the last presentation, plan to meet with group for
                         POST MORTEM (after the death).
                      Each cast and crew member writes an evaluation. Then ex-
                         change orally experiences regarding audiences and shows.

Name _____

Part _____

1. Why is stylized movement important in Children's Theater?

2. List three characters or props that make the audience use their
    imagination. In what way would they have to use their imagination?

3. What did you like the most? The least?

Comments or drawing:

MUSICAL PLAY

SUNDAY, OCTOBER 20, 1968

2:00 p.m.
Gymnasium

Children: .50¢
Adults: $1.00

RUMPELSTILTSKIN, a musical play

Suggestions for flyers and tickets,

set plans,

sound,

movement,

and songs.

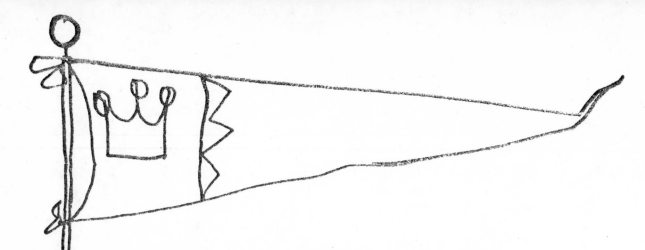

SUNDAY, OCTOBER 20, 1968
2:00 p.m., Gymnasium
CHILDREN: .50¢   ADULTS: $1.00

College of the Holy Names
3500 Mountain Boulevard
Oakland, California 94619

college of the holy names presents

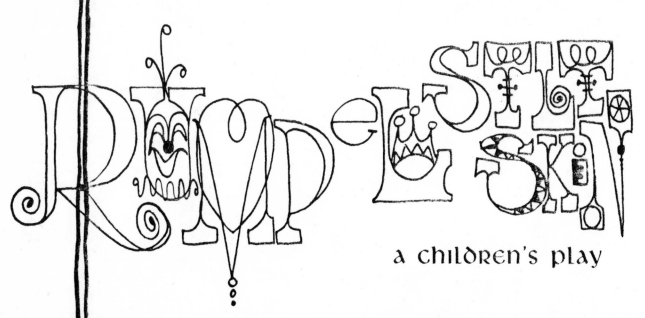

a children's play

RUMPELSTILTSKIN   Music/song

Live accompaniment: piano; or piano, violin, drums (or more instruments)
    or
Taped accompaniment: make several so that individuals may rehearse at their
                     own convenience.

SITUATION: The Princess tries to guess Rumpelstiltskin's name.

    Rumpelstiltskin: YOU CAN'T GUESS MY NAME

        Body movement: Crouched over so he looks very small
          Broad,   Hands on hips: point finger at Princess for "you"
          Stylized,   Several turn-arounds on "Search the earth..."
          Hold   Rock body back and forth while humming or
                          "ta-ta-taing" _____ is what they call me.
                        Finger to forehead on "Think..."
                        Hold imaginary book: "Use the latest dictionary"
                        Both fingers to head: "You'll just get an aching
                        brain"

    Princess: Hand under or to her chin while she things: "Is it..."
                        Both arms out: whenever she gives a name

    Rumpelstiltskin: Laughs uproariously -- picks up one leg then the other
                        as he hops about crouched over when she does not guess
                        the correct name. Broad, stylized movements always.

    Ladies in Waiting and Guard: facial and body movements should be very
                        stylized; eyes and mouth react to words spoken and
                        lines listened to.
                        Body movement: precise positions; quick exits and
                        entrances.

HOW DO YOU LIKE THAT NAME? Sung to audience, either by members of the kingdom
or by Princess, if good singers are scarce. Important to enunciate words
clearly, and encourage audience to participate in chorus, if so desired.

    Movements: Hands particularly used.

Chorus: one hand extended on "you," line 1
         line 2: finger to head for "think"
         line 3: hands thrown up for "fright"
         line 4: shrug shoulders and palms held upward

Verses: Body takes position of animal mentioned:

    Frog: crouched on rock; hop from pad to pad when name
             (Waddely-Bok) is sung.

    Moose: facial expression; arms up for horns; then play
             violin vigorously as name (Daffydumdiddle) is
             sung.

    Cock: strut; bow and waltz with hen; jig-up dancing as
             name is mentioned (Jigajogjen).

    Dragon: opened eyes: crawl up to tea table; eat fancifully
             as name (Smokeyteehee) is sung.

    Mole: swim underwater, come up for air; duck down when
             name (Doduckedin) is sung.

    Elf: quick movements among characters; dance step when
             name (Tweedletytoes) is sung.

    Zebra: two take zebra form; stroll sideways when name
             (Zeezizzerzeen) is sung.

    Cat: sit cross-legged; write in book; sign when name
             (Meeminnymigs) is sung.

All or some of verses are sung. Sometimes animals may use one side of
platform, then center, then other side, and run down in front of audience.
Variety is needed so that music, words, and movement attract and sustain
interest.

You Can't Guess My Name

you can't guess my name —— Scan the skies in vain

search the earth a thou-sand years you can't guess my name

— — — — — — 's what they call me — Think with all your might and main

use the lat-est dic - tion ar - y you'll just get an ache — ing

brain.

YOU CAN'T GUESS MY NAME

You can't guess my name
Scan the skies in vain
Search the earth a thousand years
You can't guess my name
_____ is what they call me
Think with all your might and main
Use the latest dictionary
You'll just get an aching brain

Princess: Is is...

                   Is it...Meaneymug?

          Is it...Nudnick?

                   Is it...is it Ingerpatch?

Rumpelstiltskin: (Laughs uproariously and sings chorus of song again.
                   Then exits with followers, shouting.) I warned you, I warned
                   you. You'll never guess. Never! One chance and only two to
                   go! (Laughs as he exits down the aisle.)

Princess: Oh, dear, what shall I do? I have no more names left in my head.

Lady in Waiting: Maybe we could help think of some, Your Highness.

Princess: Yes, of course, that's it. I'll ask everybody in the castle
                   and the village to help me think of names! Quickly, you run
                   all through the castle, and you run to the village and ask
                   everyone you see to come here and help me think!

Ladies: Yes, Your Highness (run off).

Princess: Guard! (guard enters) Bring me a pen and a royal scroll.
                   (Guard bows, exits)

                   (Music for names song starts in background as people begin
                   entering. She rushes to first one who enters.)

                   Do you know any unusual names? It's very important for me to find
                   the right one to fit someone I know. Please think very hard. (By
                   this time the room is full of people all buzzing excitedly.)

                   (Guard rushes in with long scroll and exaggerated pen.)

                   All right. If you'll please just tell me one at a time I can write
                   them down. (Song and dance, "How do you Like That Name" in which
                   different people sing different verses suggesting a name, and all
                   joint in to sing chorus after each verse. Exaggerated business.)

OR

                   (Princess sings song to audience and audience participates in
                   chorus.)

67

HOW DO YOU LIKE THAT NAME

Chorus: How do you like that name,
           Do you think it's the right one
           Isn't it enough to fright one
           How do you like that name?

Verses: I once knew a frog that lived on a rock
           They told me his name was Waddely-Bok.
                              Chorus.

I heard of a moose told time by the clock
They hold me his name was Noodeltytock.
                              Chorus.

There once was a mouse who played on the fiddle
The mice baby called her Daffydymiddle.
                              Chorus.

I once saw a cock who waltzed with a hen
The farmer had names him Jigajogjen.
                              Chorus.

A dragon I know liked biscuits and tea
He's called by the name of Smokeyteehee.
                              Chorus.

There once was a mole just learning to swim
I heard that his name was Doduckeldin.
                              Chorus.

I once knew an elf whose home was a rose
He told me his name was Tweedletytoes.
                              Chorus.

A zebra I saw was pink stripped with green
His mother had names him Zeezizzerzeen.
                              Chorus.

A cat that I know wrote books just for pigs
At the end he would sign them Meeminnymigs.
                              Chorus.

Audience participation in singing the Chorus may be elicited
after two or three renditions.

How Do You Like That Name

I Once knew a frog that lived on a rock They told me His name- wad-del-y Bok How do you like that name Do you think it's the right one is-n't it e-nough to fright one How do you like that name

Music by Sr. Denis, I H M
Lyrics by Sr. Marie Fleurette, I H M

Suggestions for stage set, props

Stage sets, props and makeup may be very exciting creations. Ninety percent
of the frustration lies in careful preparations. Follow the suggested hints
to ease the anxiety.

Hints on buying: Some basic equipment that may be re-used:

paint brushes
nails   Standard Brand Paints, Inc.
some paints   local hardware stores

latex paints   washes out by water
poster paints

spray paints   use outdoors only

enamel paints   washes out by turpentine or acetone (not
                               recommended for use by small children;
                               proper ventilation is a "must" when using
                               solvents)

cardboard and   ask around -- many of these things one can
other props   get free -- all for the asking and picking
                               up!

printing of posters, programs, and tickets can be done inexpensively
by instant offset printing companies. Set up the exact size of design
on white paper using black ink, leaving a ½-inch margin all around.
(One can save $15 - $30 by doing one's own pasteup job.) There may be
parents of children in the school who are printers. It is worth asking
their assistance!

A word of advice for those unsure of their creativity in designing sets:
    Be simple and let the acting be outstanding.
    The props and the stage sets are only successful in as far as the
      dramatization is well done.
    The play is not an art exhibit!

Ask students in upper grades, or employ students from art departments in local
colleges; they may have excellent creative abilities.

Finally: Look first to the talent in your own group!

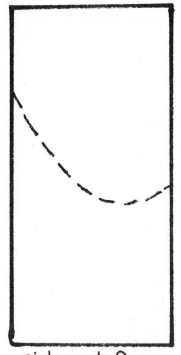

side cut for
arms of throne

back of throne

directions
for making
the King's
throne

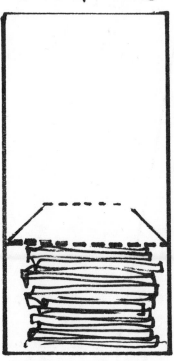

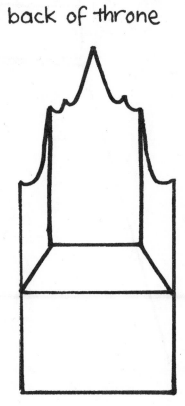

fold along dotted
lines into the
box construction
to make seat.
fill inside with
newspapers to
make seat sturdy.

71

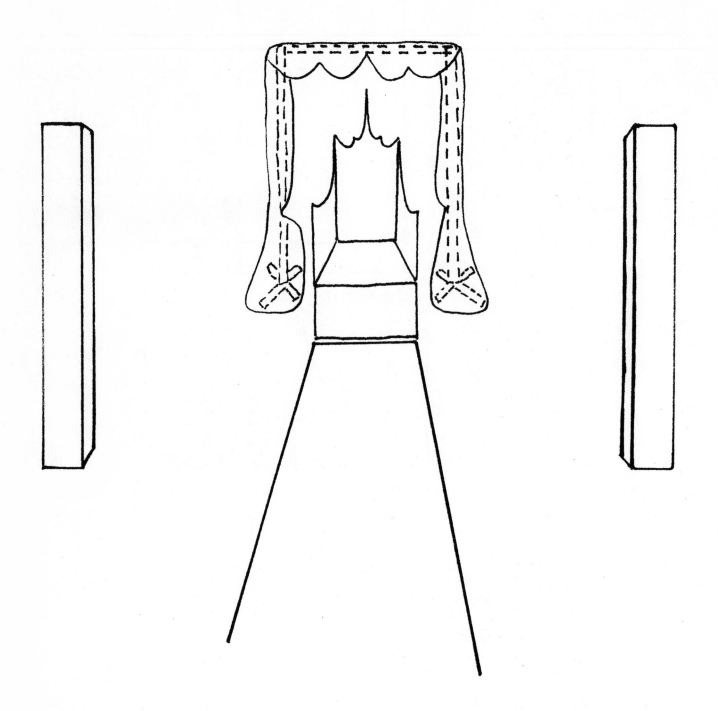

MATERIALS

Boxes

Much may be said for a box!

Familiarize yourself with its possibilities:

   a box can surround, hide, cover, or store objects
   a box can contain or house items
   a box can divide space
   a box can isolate objects
   a box can be decorated, painted, or cut out
   a box can be used to sit upon, sit at
   a box can be lifted up in the air, carried, or buried in the
      ground
   a box can be worn as a dress or a pair of shoes or can sit upon
      the head as a crown or hat

Think of the many, many ways a box may be used in a production!

Whatever you use a box for, you most likely want others to notice
it. The shape and decoration on the box have a lot to say for what it
is as a prop.

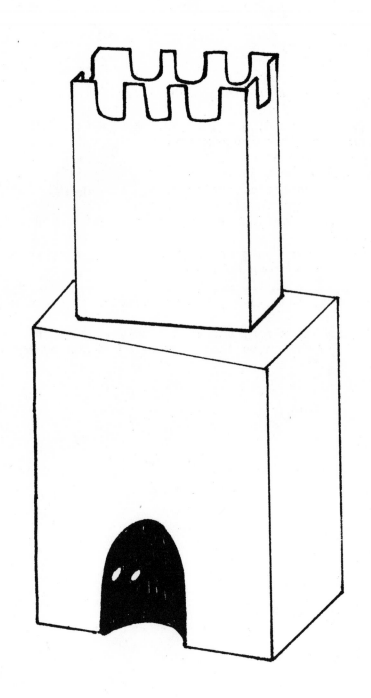

PAINTING

In classrooms: use water base paints, such as:
     poster paint
     acrylic paints
     water color paints
     chalk
     white latex paints

   **Use water base paints; paintbrushes are easy to keep clean and wear
longer.**

   If you have large areas to cover, do not hesitate to have brushes
three inches wide and smaller for narrower lines.

     Clean up with water:
          poster paints
          acrylic paints
          water colors
          chalks

     Clean up with paint thinners, turpentine, acetone (not recommended
around children):
          oil base paints
          enamel paints

   As with the use of any paints, particular attention is paid to the
proper ventilation. Essential at all times! Very important to the health
and safety of everyone!

   Before actual painting begins provide several disposable containers,
newspapers, and rags -- all available in the work room.

   Cover the floor with newspapers -- much less work to do in clean-up
later!

   After clean-up, empty all wastebaskets into outdoor trash facilities.
Do not let oily rags or newspapers remain in building over night, or even
for several hours.

STAGE DESIGNING

Oftentimes the idea of designing a stage is frightening, because of our associations with the big Broadway stages, movies and television. Those working in drama with the young beginners must remind and alert themselves to this fact: children's theater not only offers the opportunity for children to express themselves bodily and verbally, to bring wonder and delight to an audience which, hopefully, will respond with appreciation and applause, but it also provides the framework within which children may explore their talents and increase their awareness of other so-called technical contributions to a production -- namely, props and sets.

Props and backdrops for scenes can be effective in complementing the acting. The following are some suggestions which are simple and inexpensive to plan and execute, yet attractive and stylish.

USE OF SLIDES OFFER VARIED TECHNIQUES IN SILHOUETTING OR COLORED SCENERY:

Purchase slide frames from a camera shop. Cut clear plastic to fit the frame. Draw design with india ink or plastic ink on the plastic. Encase in the frame. Ready -- project!

For a colored scene, cut out small pictures from magazines, such as Life and Woman's Day. (Not all magazine pictures work, as the outcome depends upon the type of ink used in printing.) Adhere clear contact paper to the picture; soak it in turpentine. (Some pictures just require that they be soaked in water.) The paper should pull away from the plastic leaving the ink print on the plastic. Dry. Cut to fit in the slide frame.

With a 35 mm. camera, take pictures of scenery or of characters in the play. Project these pictures as part of the backdrop.

FRONT PROJECTION is the best way to project these slides to an audience. Hang a sheet as a backdrop on the stage.

Project in back of the sheet.

This setup has two primary advantages: no cords need clutter the audience aisles; and the audience has unblocked vision of the stage.

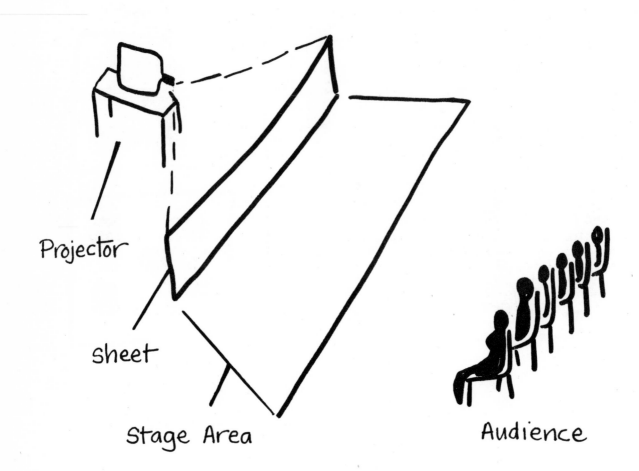

Projector

Sheet

Stage Area

Audience

Most producers shy away from reusing designs more than once. It can be done, very simply using inexpensive equipment. Draw a pattern or design on a piece of heavy butcher paper, or on cardboard. Cut out the design. Varnish both sides of the cardboard or paper, and allow to dry. This procedure gives lasting value to the stencil which may be stored away and used again and again. Store the large stencil flat.

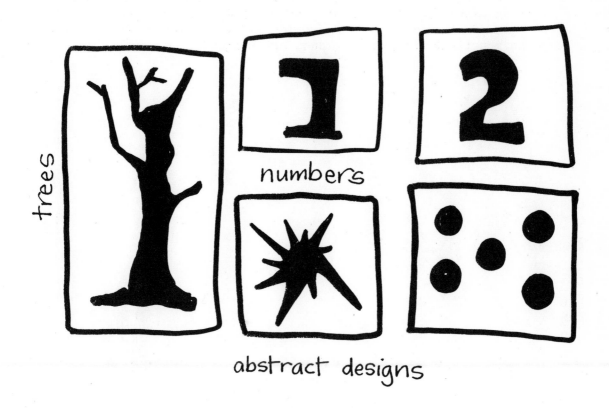

trees

numbers

abstract designs

For a multiple display of sporadic color, crumple large sheets of butcher
paper. Spray with one color; let dry; crumple again and spray with
another color. Two to four colors are suggested. Stretch out the large
sheets of paper by spraying with water and lay flat to dry outdoors.
After it is dry, it is ready for use!

     For tie-dye or painting scenery as a background display: use sheets,
muslin, or drapery material. Commercial dyes may be used. If so, the
same material may be used for another scene. Directions: soak material
fairly clean in Clorax. Poster paint washes out in soap and water. This
procedure makes it possible to use the material over several times, there-
by helping on the financial end, if funds are scarce or not available.